SUN, MOON & STARS

By Michael S. Buhl

Illustrated by Hans G. Schellenberger with cartoons by Angelika Stubner

Translated from the German and edited by M. Spurgeon

Brown Watson

ENGLAND

Title of the original German edition:
Mein erstes Frage- und Antwortbuch
Sonne, Mond und Sterne
© 1997 Loewe Verlag GmbH, Bindlach

English edition first published in 2000 by
Brown Watson, The Old Mill,
Kibworth Beauchamp,
Leicestershire LE8 0HG, England

© 2000 English edition, Brown Watson

ISBN: 0-7097-1336-3

Printed in the E.C.

Contents

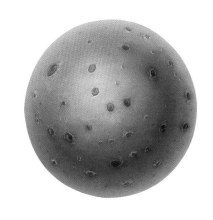

How did the Universe begin?

Scientists who observe the stars are called astronomers. They believe that the Universe began with a giant ball of matter exploding in space. This explosion is known as the 'Big Bang' and it happened about 15,000 million years ago, millions and millions of years before life began on Earth.

After the 'Big Bang' huge clouds of gas spread into space. Some of these clouds began to roll into hot, thick balls of shining gas. This is how the stars were formed.

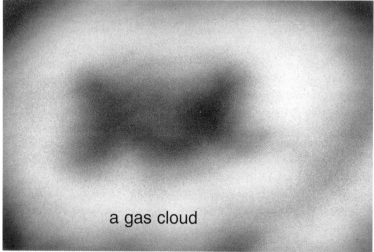

a gas cloud

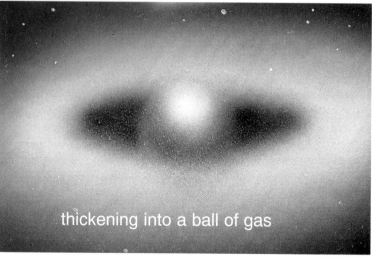

thickening into a ball of gas

How does a star die?

Sometimes, when all the fuel in a star has been used up, it sinks into itself and burns out in a powerful explosion. This is called a Supernova. Other stars swell out into huge, red fireballs called 'red giants'. Gradually a red giant loses its outer layer, leaving only the core. This shines clear and bright, but is much smaller than the original star. This core is known as a 'white dwarf' because it is small and white.

Star

Red Giant

White Dwarf

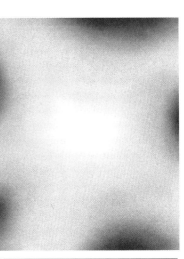

Supernova

A clear, shining Supernova being studied from an observatory.

Where is the Earth?

If astronauts were to travel through the Universe in a space ship, they would see the Earth as it is shown below, surrounded by thousands and thousands of stars. This collection of stars, or galaxy, is known as the Milky Way.

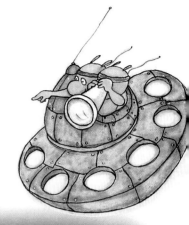

Andromeda Galaxy

Milky Way

Each clear dot is a sun. The small circle shows the position of our Sun. The Earth is too small to be seen on this scale.

Why is our galaxy called the Milky Way?

Our galaxy actually forms a spiral, as you can see in this picture. Because the Earth is at the centre of the galaxy, we see it as a milky-white band across the sky. This is why the Ancient Greeks called it 'The Milky Way'.

The arrow points to our Solar System.

This is how the Milky Way would look if we could see it sideways.

Many of the stars that we can see are really no longer there. They died a long time ago. What we are seeing is their light. There are also new stars that we cannot yet see, because their light has not yet reached the Earth. Light can take years to travel the vast distances of the Universe.

How many stars are there?

The stars which we can see in the sky are only a small proportion of the countless stars in the Universe. Astronomers have calculated that there are at least 100 billion stars in the Milky Way alone – and there are many other galaxies in the Universe apart from the Milky Way!

Astronomers have discovered well over 200 million galaxies in the Universe so far.

a giant star

What is a comet?

A comet is a great lump of ice and dust, which is why they are sometimes known as 'dirty snowballs'. Some comets have a diameter of only a few kilometres, while others measure 10 kilometres or more. Comets orbit the Sun, gravitating towards it. As a comet nears the Sun, the ice evaporates, leaving a tail of vapour trailing behind.

gas and dust breaking free

comet nucleus

the comet's tail

What are meteors and meteorites?

A meteor is a great chunk of stone or iron, or a mixture of both. Most meteors burn out as they fly through the Universe. As they get closer to the Earth, some explode and pieces fall to the ground as meteorites.

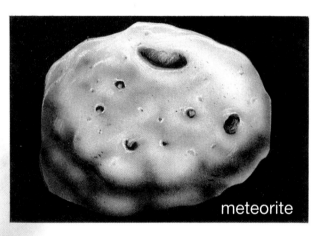

meteorite

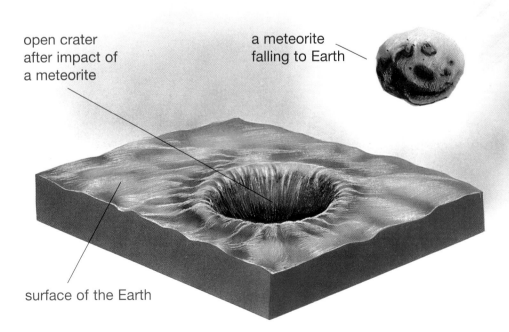

open crater
after impact of
a meteorite

a meteorite
falling to Earth

surface of the Earth

What is the Solar System?

There are many suns. When heavenly bodies are attracted towards a sun and begin to move around it, together they form a solar system. The path of each heavenly body is called an orbit. A heavenly body orbiting a sun is a planet. A heavenly body orbiting a planet is a satellite, which we refer to as a moon.

What does our Solar System look like?

Our Earth is a planet. It belongs to a solar system and, like the eight other planets in the system, orbits the Sun. At the time of the 'Big Bang' it exploded through the Universe at an estimated speed of 107,000 kilometres per hour, a hundred times faster than a jet aircraft. When the Earth has moved once around the Sun, a year has passed. Each planet follows its own orbit. On the picture below, you can also see a band of small specks between the orbits of Mars and Jupiter. This is called the Asteroid Belt and it is made up of millions of rocks.

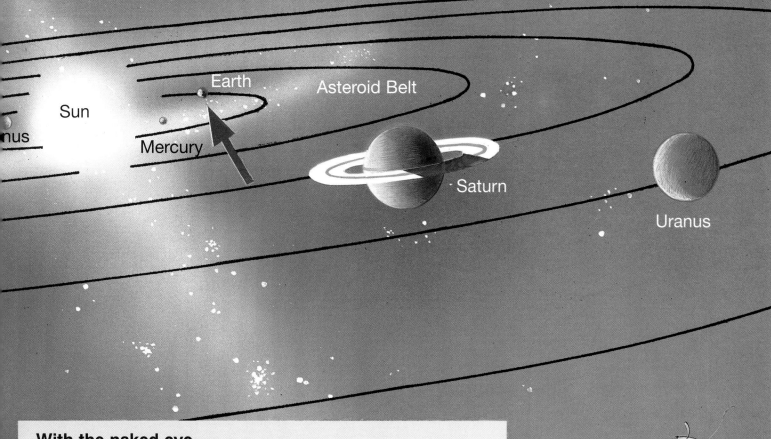

Sun

Earth

Asteroid Belt

Mercury

Saturn

Uranus

With the naked eye

Many planets can be seen quite easily with the naked eye. Venus appears clearly, shining with a bluish light. Jupiter shines with a clear, yellow light. Mars gleams with a reddish tinge in the sky, and Saturn blue-grey. Planets have no light of their own. They get light from the Sun and also from the stars. So when you see these planets, you know that it is because the Sun is shining on them and not because they are shining on their own.

Why do we need the Sun?

Without the Sun it would always be dark on Earth and everything would be ice-cold and rigid. Our planet would be lifeless, with no people, no plants and no animals. The Sun gives us our light. No wonder that for centuries people in ancient times worshipped the Sun as a god, a divine being. Today, we know that our Sun is a star, which sheds its light and releases its energy for us, warming the Earth with its rays.

The Pharaoh Ikhnaton (or Akhenaton) worshipped the Sun as a god.

Sunspots are powerful whirlwinds of gas. The wind makes their temperature lower than that of the Sun, so they appear black on the surface.

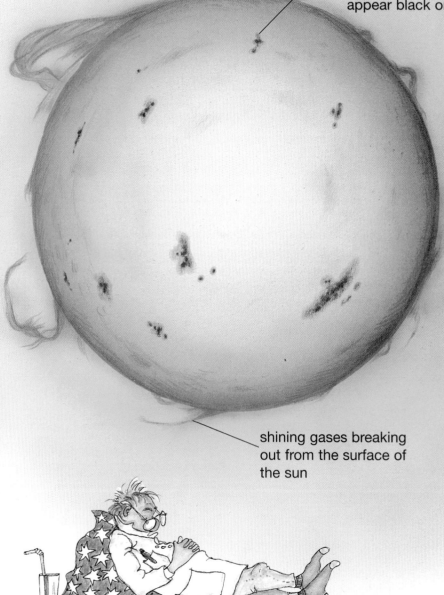

shining gases breaking out from the surface of the sun

Section from an Egyptian limestone carving, dating from about 1370 B.C.

How hot is the Sun?

Our Sun is a glowing, hot ball of gas. Its temperature is millions of degrees Celcius at its centre. At its surface, it is about 5,900° Celcius. If it were possible for a piece of the Sun, no bigger than a football, to be brought to Earth, nobody would be able to get anywhere near it because of the heat.

5900°
500000°
1000000°
2000000°
5000000°
10000000°
15000000°

Earth's orbit

Position of the Earth

Position of the Earth

Maximum distance from Sun

Minimum distance from Sun

152.1m km

147.1m km

on 6 July

on 2 January

The Earth moves in an ellipse (oval) around the Sun.

Earth's orbit

How far is the Sun from the Earth?

It is about 150 million kilometres from the Earth to the Sun or eight light minutes. This means that the light rays from the Sun take about eight minutes to reach the Earth. If the Earth's orbit were nearer to the Sun, everything would wither in the heat. If it were further from the Sun, our planet would soon be covered with ice.

Sun

The Sun is more than 100 times larger than the Earth. There are suns in the Universe which are even bigger.

Earth

What is the 'Man in the Moon'?

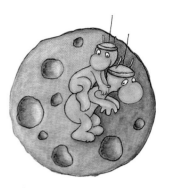

With a little imagination, we can look at a full Moon and see the face of a man with wide, staring eyes and an open mouth! This picture is formed by the dark spots on the Moon's surface. These 'spots' are actually craters and valleys, made by meteors and meteorites crashing down on its surface. The first astronomers believed that these spots were seas and lakes, which is why they are still known as 'seas' today.

Sea of Tranquility

Seas of Crises

crater

section of the Moon's surface

During the day, it is quite hot on the Moon (about 130° Celsius). At night, it is icy-cold, (minus 150° Celsius).

The Moon has no atmosphere and no air to breathe. There is also no water on the Moon and this is why nothing grows there.

How big is the Moon?

The Moon has a diameter of 3478 kilometres and is much smaller than the Earth. There is also much less gravity on the Moon. This means that on the Moon we could jump six times higher than on the Earth.

lunar module

The astronauts explore the area around the lunar module.

On 20 July 1969 the American Space Mission Apollo 11 landed on the Moon. Neil Armstrong became the first man to set foot on the Moon.

How far away is the Moon?

The Earth is about 384,000 kilometres from the Moon. If you wanted to travel the same distance on the Earth, you would have to fly around the world ten times.

The Moon's orbit of the Earth is not a perfect circle. The Moon appears bigger when it is nearer to the Earth.

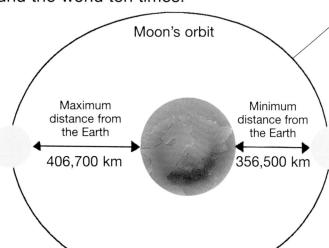

Moon's orbit

Maximum distance from the Earth

406,700 km

Minimum distance from the Earth

356,500 km

Why does the Moon appear bigger and smaller?

The Moon does, of course, stay the same size and does not actually get any bigger or smaller. As it orbits the Earth, we see only the part of the Moon on which the Sun is shining. When the Moon spins on its axis towards the Earth, its nearside is not lit up by the Sun, and so we only see a small part of the Moon. When this happens we say it is a 'new Moon'.

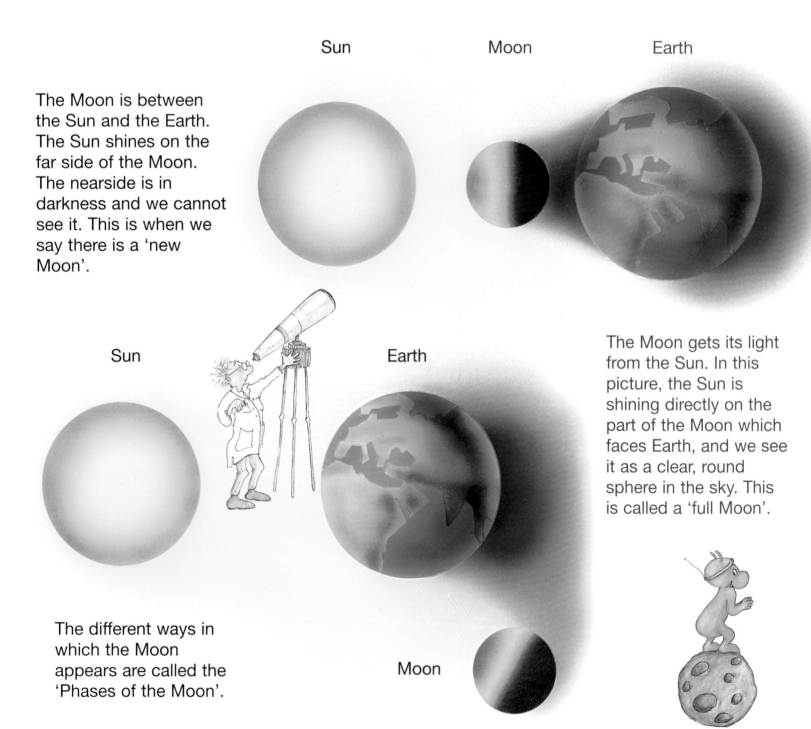

The Moon is between the Sun and the Earth. The Sun shines on the far side of the Moon. The nearside is in darkness and we cannot see it. This is when we say there is a 'new Moon'.

The Moon gets its light from the Sun. In this picture, the Sun is shining directly on the part of the Moon which faces Earth, and we see it as a clear, round sphere in the sky. This is called a 'full Moon'.

The different ways in which the Moon appears are called the 'Phases of the Moon'.

How long does the Moon's orbit last?

The Moon takes about 28 days to orbit the Earth. In ancient times, people divided the year into 'moons'. The Moon's orbit was a 'lunar month', and we get the word 'month' from 'moon'.

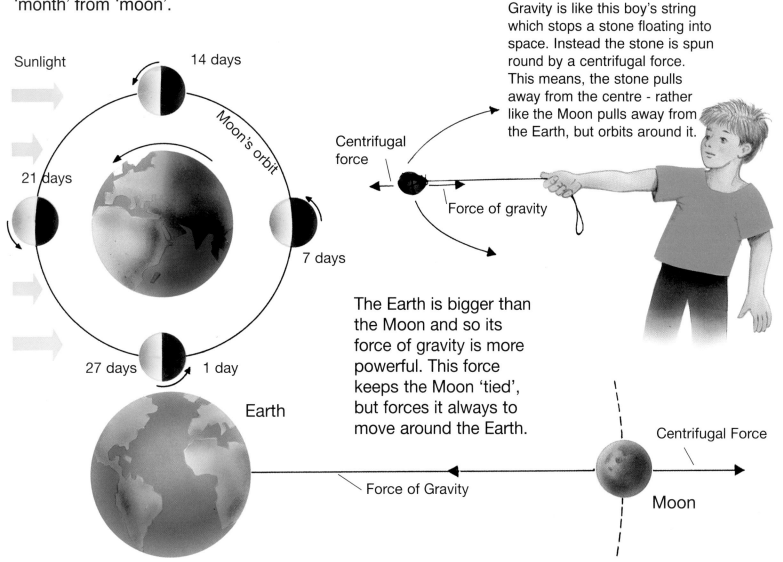

Sunlight

14 days

Moon's orbit

21 days

7 days

27 days

1 day

Earth

Gravity is like this boy's string which stops a stone floating into space. Instead the stone is spun round by a centrifugal force. This means, the stone pulls away from the centre - rather like the Moon pulls away from the Earth, but orbits around it.

Centrifugal force

Force of gravity

The Earth is bigger than the Moon and so its force of gravity is more powerful. This force keeps the Moon 'tied', but forces it always to move around the Earth.

Force of Gravity

Centrifugal Force

Moon

Why do we always see the same side of the Moon?

As the Moon spins on its own axis, so the Earth spins on its axis at the same time. Because the Earth and the Moon spin at exactly the same rate, we always see the same side of the Moon.

far side of the Moon

near side of the Moon

What is an eclipse?

When the Moon lies directly between the Sun and the Earth, a dark disk covers the Sun. A shadow is cast over the Earth. For three or four minutes, day is as dark as night. Then the Moon moves a little more, and the Sun appears again. We call this a Solar Eclipse.

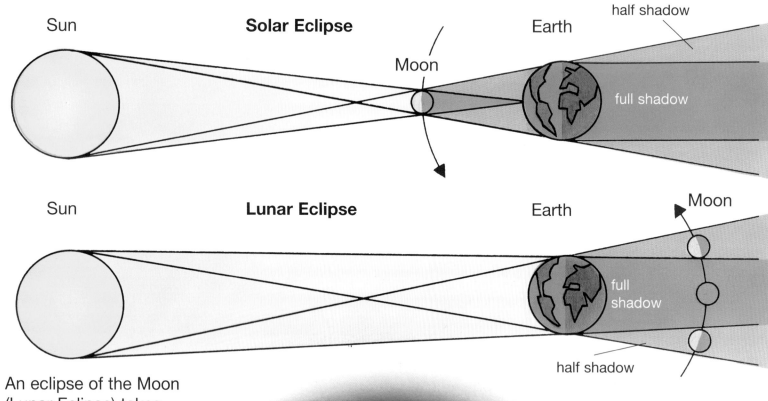

Solar Eclipse

Sun · Moon · Earth · half shadow · full shadow

Lunar Eclipse

Sun · Earth · Moon · full shadow · half shadow

An eclipse of the Moon (Lunar Eclipse) takes place when the Earth comes between the Sun and the Moon. The shadow of the Earth falls across the Moon.

During a Lunar Eclipse, the Moon can still be seen, but is bathed in a coppery-coloured light.

How does the Moon control the tides?

The rise and fall of the sea is known as the tides. An ebb tide is when the water level drops and the sea appears to be moving away from the coastline. With a flood tide the water level rises and the water appears to come back to the coastline. The tides change about every six hours and it is all due to the pull of gravity from the Moon.

Ebb

Flood

The Moon is smaller than the Earth and because of this has less gravity. However, the Moon's gravity is enough to pull the waters of our seas and large rivers. This pull of gravity causes what some people call the 'flood mountain'. This is about 70 cms high and it draws water away from the level of the seas so that we get an ebb tide. Then, as the Earth turns, the Moon's gravity means that 'flood mountain' moves away from us. The water level returns and we get a flood tide.

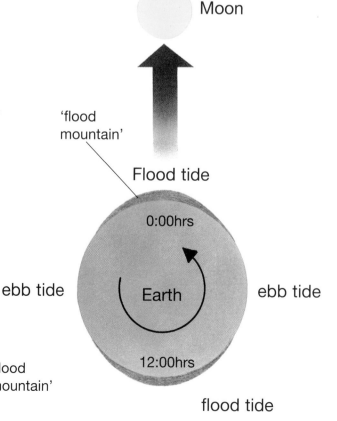

Moon

'flood mountain'

Flood tide

0:00hrs

ebb tide · Earth · ebb tide

12:00hrs

flood tide

About once a week, the 'flood mountain' is horizontal.

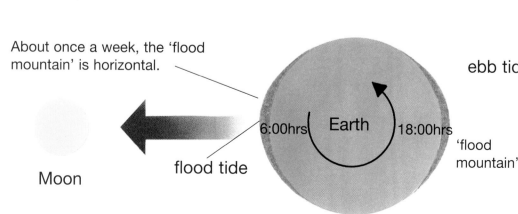

Moon

flood tide

6:00hrs · Earth · 18:00hrs

'flood mountain'

How many inner planets are there?

The planets within the Asteroid Belt – Mercury, Venus, Mars, and our own planet, Earth – are called the Inner Planets. The other planets in the Solar System are called the Outer Planets because they are outside the Asteroid Belt.

Mercury

This planet is named after the Roman god, Mercury. It has the fastest orbit in the Solar System, and takes only 88 days to travel around the Sun. The whole planet is pitted with craters, like the Moon. On Mercury it would be unbearably hot by day and icy cold at night.

Mercury is the nearest planet to the Sun.

The surface is solid, but desolate and bare.

craters

Venus

Venus is almost as large as the Earth. It is surrounded by a thick layer of cloud. For a long time it was believed that people could live there. Then it was discovered that it was unbearably hot underneath the layer of cloud. Also there are many volcanoes which spit out glowing rocks.

The American space probe Magellan just missing the surface of Venus.

Mars

This planet takes its name from the Roman god of war, because it glows blood red. The surface of Mars contains a lot of iron which, in the course of time, has become rusty – hence the red colour! This planet is smaller than Earth, but it has two moons and the highest mountain in the whole of the Solar System. There could never be any human life on this planet, because it is so very hot by day and unbearably cold at night. In addition, the air is too thin to breathe.

The highest mountain on Mars is 27,000 metres high.

What are the Outer Planets?

We already know something about the four Inner Planets (Mercury, Venus, Earth and Mars). Now let's move on to the other five planets (Jupiter, Saturn, Uranus, Neptune and Pluto). But, before we do, we must first go through the Asteroid Belt!

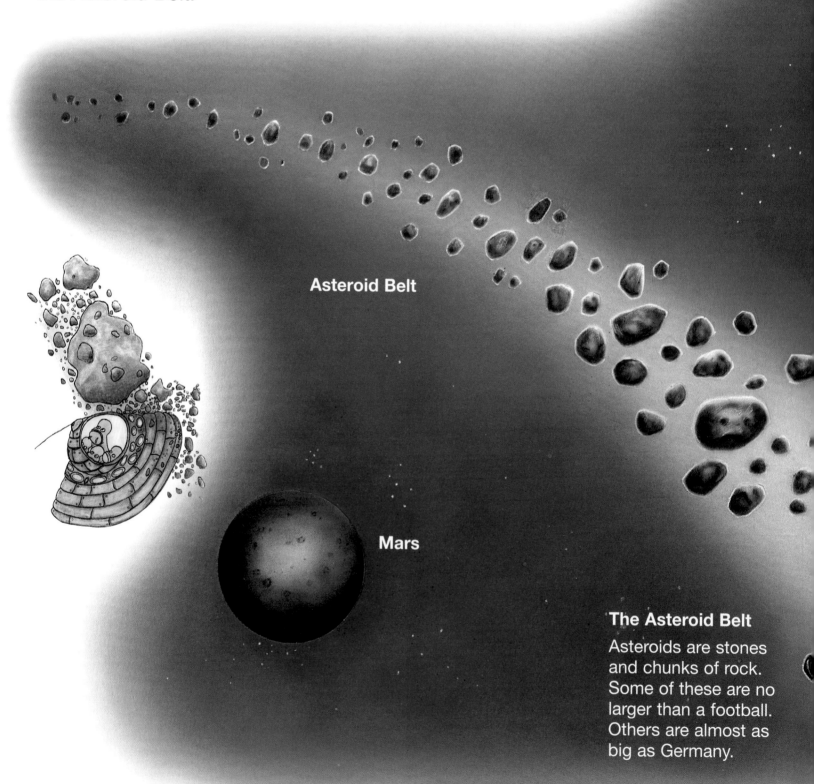

Asteroid Belt

Mars

The Asteroid Belt
Asteroids are stones and chunks of rock. Some of these are no larger than a football. Others are almost as big as Germany.

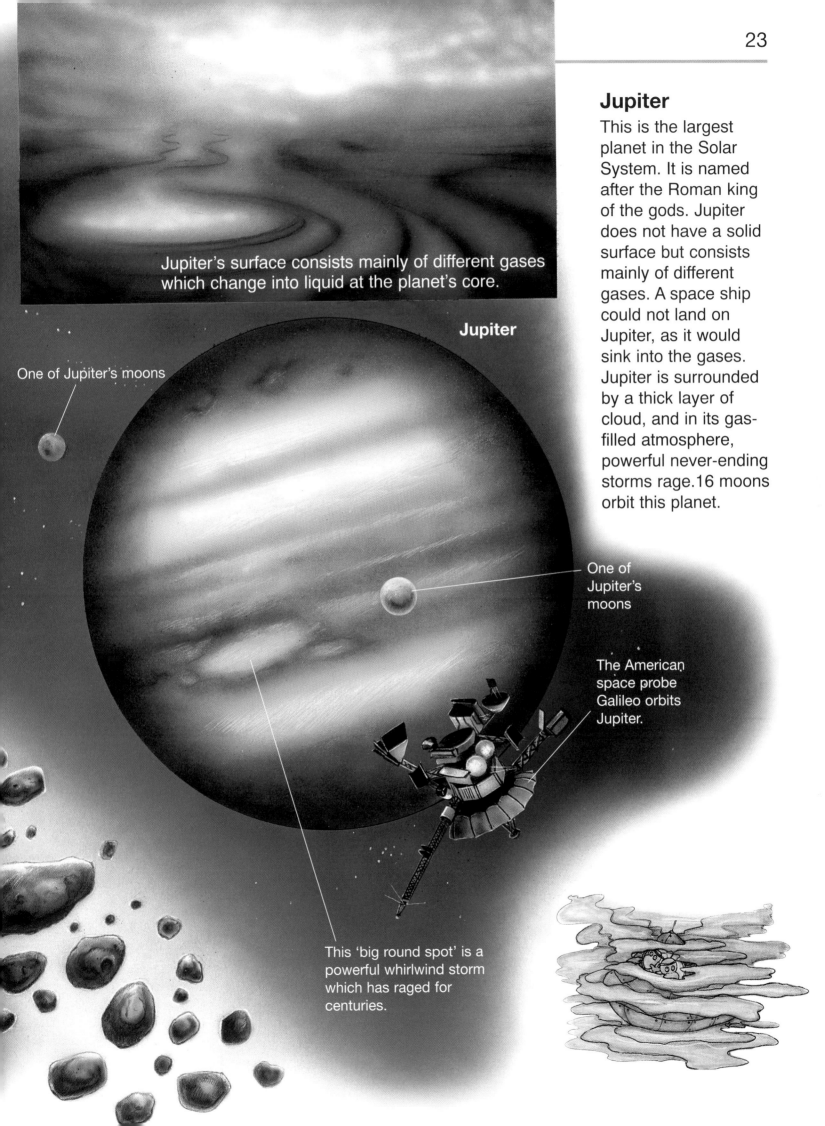

Jupiter's surface consists mainly of different gases which change into liquid at the planet's core.

Jupiter

One of Jupiter's moons

Jupiter

This is the largest planet in the Solar System. It is named after the Roman king of the gods. Jupiter does not have a solid surface but consists mainly of different gases. A space ship could not land on Jupiter, as it would sink into the gases. Jupiter is surrounded by a thick layer of cloud, and in its gas-filled atmosphere, powerful never-ending storms rage.16 moons orbit this planet.

One of Jupiter's moons

The American space probe Galileo orbits Jupiter.

This 'big round spot' is a powerful whirlwind storm which has raged for centuries.

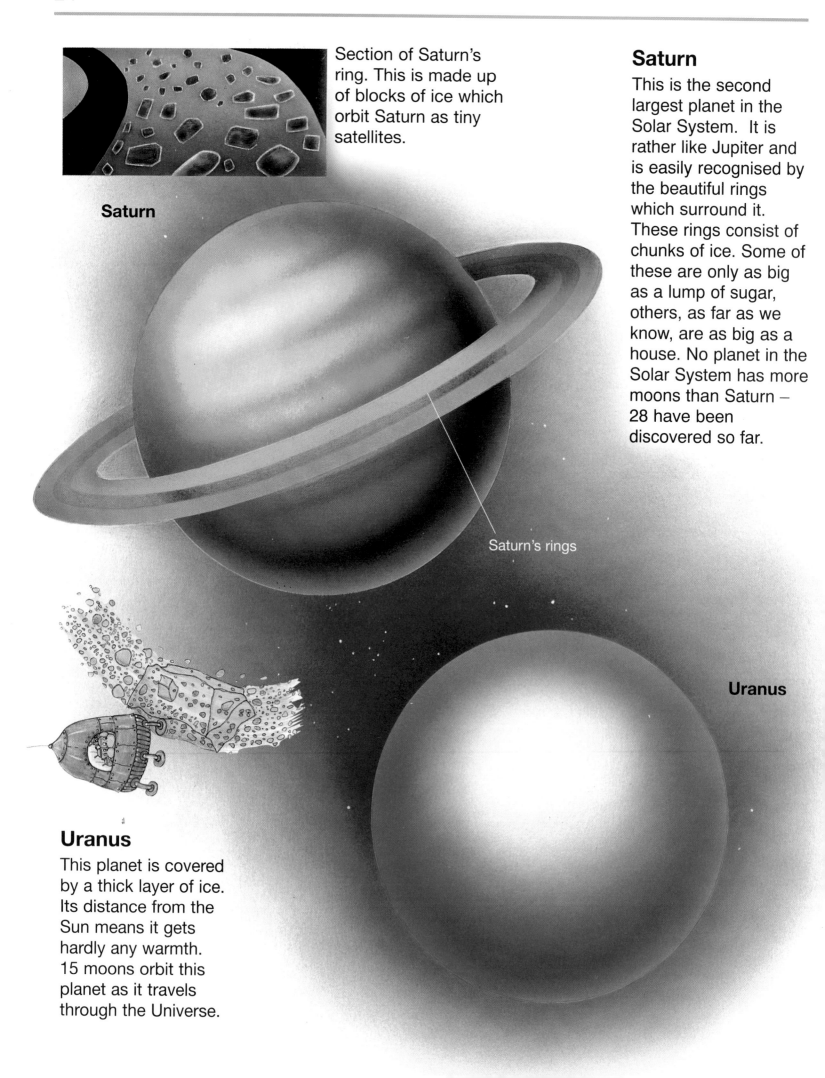

Section of Saturn's ring. This is made up of blocks of ice which orbit Saturn as tiny satellites.

Saturn

Saturn

This is the second largest planet in the Solar System. It is rather like Jupiter and is easily recognised by the beautiful rings which surround it. These rings consist of chunks of ice. Some of these are only as big as a lump of sugar, others, as far as we know, are as big as a house. No planet in the Solar System has more moons than Saturn – 28 have been discovered so far.

Saturn's rings

Uranus

Uranus

This planet is covered by a thick layer of ice. Its distance from the Sun means it gets hardly any warmth. 15 moons orbit this planet as it travels through the Universe.

Pluto is more than 5.9 billion kilometres from the Sun.

Size comparison of Pluto and the Earth

Pluto

Earth

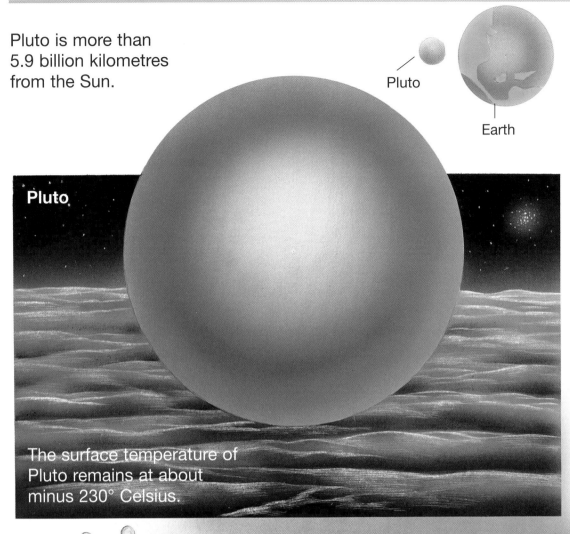

Pluto

The surface temperature of Pluto remains at about minus 230° Celsius.

Pluto

Pluto was the Roman god of wealth, as well as of the underworld. This planet is the smallest in the Solar System. It is also the furthest from the Sun and is far colder than we could imagine. Like the Earth, Pluto has just one moon. It is right at the edge of our Solar System.

Neptune

Neptune was named after the Roman god of the sea and the planet really does resemble the colour of the ocean. It is as big as Uranus and, like Uranus, is covered with a thick layer of ice. 8 moons orbit this planet and there is always a powerful whirlwind raging somewhere.

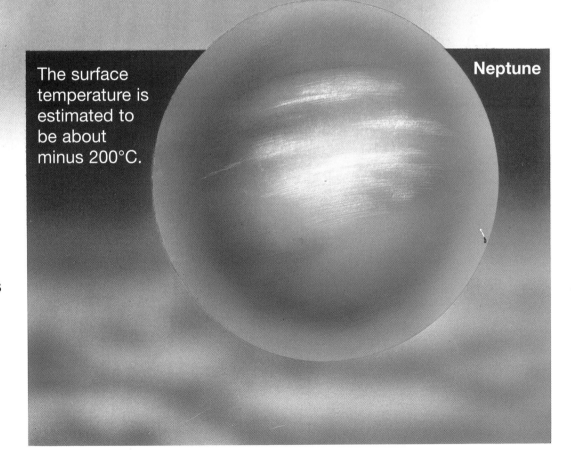

The surface temperature is estimated to be about minus 200°C.

Neptune

What was the Earth once thought to be like?

For hundreds of years, most people thought that the Sun, the planets and the stars revolved around the Earth. Throughout the centuries, however, there were men who believed that this was not true.

The Earth as a flat disc: this is how most people imagined our planet to be. In the middle of the disc was the land, with water all around it. For a very long time, men were frightened to go too far out to sea, because it was believed that they would fall off the edge.

Aristarchus

Aristarchus was a scholar of Ancient Greece who lived about 2,300 years ago. He was one of the first men who recognized that the Earth was not flat, but a globe. He claimed that the Earth moved around the Sun, but hardly anyone believed him. By the time he died, his theory had almost been forgotten.

Copernicus

About 500 years ago, Polish astronomer Nicolaus Copernicus was observing the stars and realised that Aristarchus had been right! He wrote a book about the orbit of the Earth around the Sun. In 1543, soon after it was published, Copernicus died, but he is still remembered as the founder of modern astronomy.

Isaac Newton

Nicolaus Copernicus

Galileo

About 40 years after Copernicus, Italian scientist Galileo Galilei continued to search for answers. With a powerful telescope, he discovered four of Jupiter's moons. He also proved that Venus moved around the Sun and – as Copernicus had also believed – that all the planets moved around the Sun. When he wrote a book about his discoveries, he was accused of casting doubt on the Bible. He had to withdraw his findings as the Bible says that the Sun moves around the Earth.

Newton

One year after Galileo's death, Isaac Newton was born in England. He discovered the force of gravity when he realised that an object thrown into the air fell back to the ground. This also explained why the Moon moved around the Earth instead of floating off into the Universe. The Earth kept the Moon in orbit with its own force of gravity. The Sun, being the greatest force of gravity, kept all the planets in a regular orbit.

Aristarchus, Galileo and Copernicus were right: everything in our solar system orbits the Sun.

Galileo Galilei

How far can we see into space?

In the world's observatories – these are places where scientists observe the planets and the stars – astronomers use the most powerful radio telescopes to observe stars and galaxies which are millions of kilometres away from Earth.

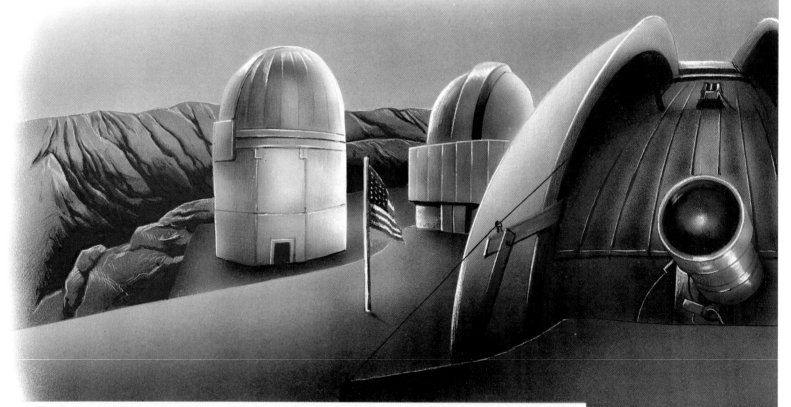

View of the great Magellan Cloud, 175,000 light years from the Earth.

Observatories are often built on high land, where the air is pure. This means astronomers can see the stars more clearly. Huge, revolving telescopes are operated beneath domes which open and close.

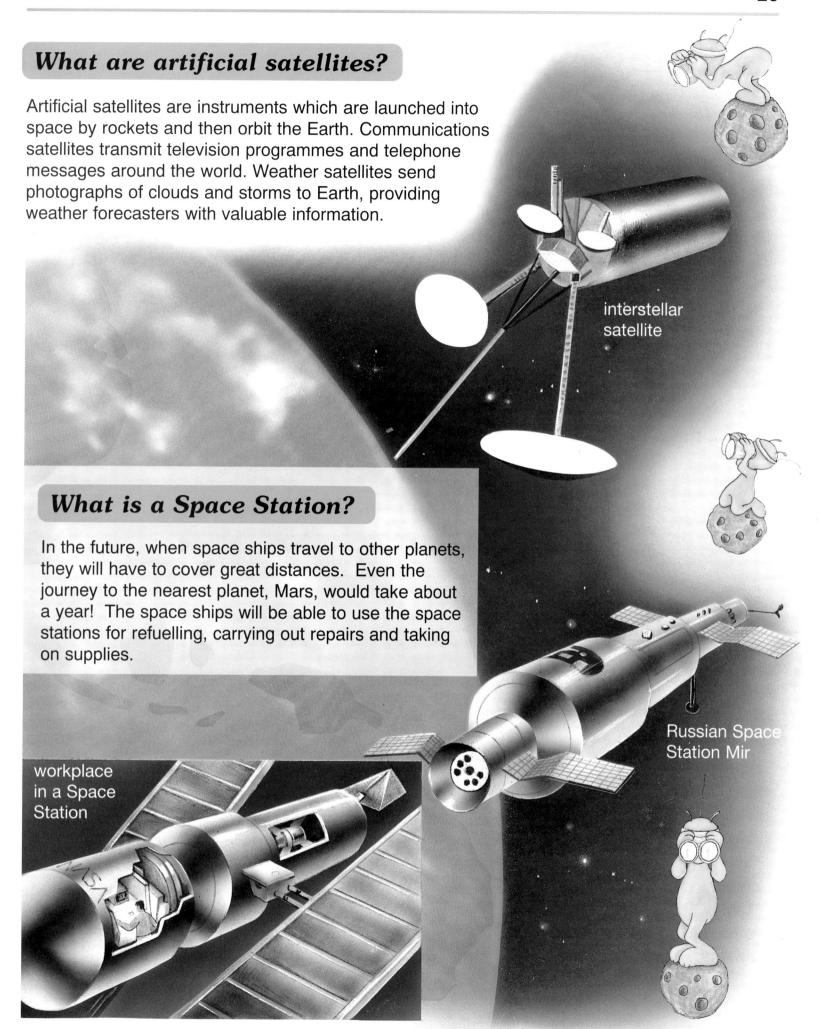

What are artificial satellites?

Artificial satellites are instruments which are launched into space by rockets and then orbit the Earth. Communications satellites transmit television programmes and telephone messages around the world. Weather satellites send photographs of clouds and storms to Earth, providing weather forecasters with valuable information.

interstellar satellite

What is a Space Station?

In the future, when space ships travel to other planets, they will have to cover great distances. Even the journey to the nearest planet, Mars, would take about a year! The space ships will be able to use the space stations for refuelling, carrying out repairs and taking on supplies.

Russian Space Station Mir

workplace in a Space Station

How much have you learnt?

Beneath each of the following pictures there is a question. How many can you answer? If you are not sure, just look for the same picture in the book!

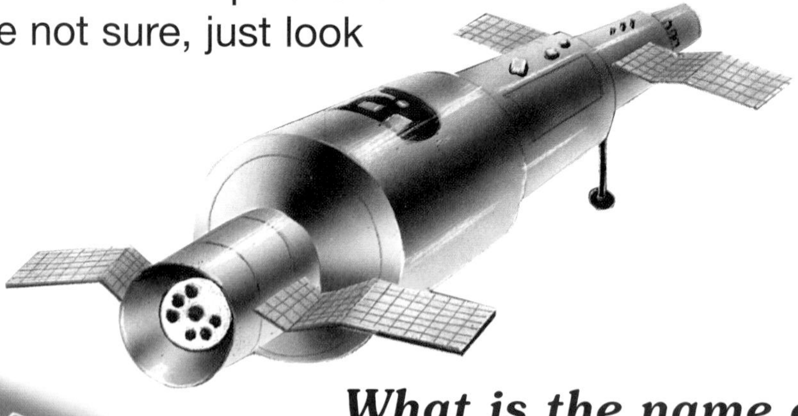

What are asteroids?

What is the name of this space station?

What is the name of this planet?

Who first realised that the Earth was not a flat disc?

What does a comet consist of?

What is the largest planet called?

Is the Earth bigger or smaller than the Moon?

What is an observatory?

What is the name of our galaxy?

Who was the first man on the Moon?

Index